To my brother Federico – my built-in
best friend, a God-given gift and
the most precious thing I have.

And to my Mum and Dad,
for giving me both roots and wings.

Soothing self-care rituals for every day

CALM

IN A

BOOK

PART 1
Intro

Feeling rested, mindful and centred
8

Things that you deserve
10

PART 2
Feeling Rested

What is rest?
14

Self-care ideas for rest
18

Overcoming guilt
34

Your rest routine
44

PART 3
Feeling Mindful

What is mindfulness?
54

Self-care for mindfulness
62

For the body
66

For the mind
74

For the soul
82

Your mindfulness routine
90

PART 4
Feeling Centred

Self-care ideas for staying centred
100

Practising gratitude
108

Your centred self-care routine
112

Embracing Imperfection
142

References
156

PART 1

intro

Hi there, and welcome! Let's dive into your ultimate self-care guide to feeling rested, mindful and centred. Let this book be your evening companion and journal to come to for a peaceful moment after a busy day.

Calm in a Book has been created to provide you with many self-care ideas and engaging activities for your mind, body and soul that can help you create more moments of calm in your life. Split into three self-care sections – feeling rested, feeling mindful and feeling centred – this book is a gentle guide to building long-term self-care habits for rest and relaxation.

In each section you can discover bite-sized research findings on the science of wellbeing, as well as guided writing exercises with journaling space to help you make these yours. If you would like to read more about the research studies we talk about, you can find a reading list at the end of the book.

Use this book to discover new ways to care for yourself and how to start using them to build daily self-care habits that prioritise your health, your needs and moments of rest without guilt. No matter how you feel or how much time you have, there will always be something in these pages to help you.

Feeling rested, mindful and centred

The self-care activities and reflective journaling exercises in this book aim to make you feel more rested, more mindful and more centred. Why should this be a goal? By working towards feeling rested, mindful and centred, you're giving yourself the space to recharge, be present and navigate life with even more ease.

♥ Feeling rested isn't just about sleep, it's about restoring your energy in ways that truly nourish you.

♥ Feeling mindful helps you to slow down and appreciate the present, rather than rushing through life on autopilot.

♥ And feeling centred means staying grounded and connected to yourself, even when things get stressful.

When these three elements come together, self-care becomes more than just a quick fix – it becomes a way of living that supports your wellbeing for the long run.

By breaking self-care into these three sections, this book offers a gentle, flexible approach to feeling more rested, mindful and centred in daily life. Instead of rigid routines or overwhelming to-do lists, it's about making small, intentional shifts; taking tiny moments of rest, mindfulness and reflection that add up over time.

THINGS THAT YOU DESERVE:

- Feeling safe
- Healing
- A home within yourself
- A love that doesn't require you to shrink
- The beauty of imperfection

- ♥ Moments of unfiltered joy
- ♥ The freedom to change your mind
- ♥ A second chance (or a third, or a fourth)
- ♥ Friendships that help you grow
- ♥ An environment that honours your individuality

PART 2
feeling rested

Feeling rested is about achieving a state of physical, mental and emotional renewal, where one feels recharged, balanced and capable of facing daily challenges. It involves more than just getting enough sleep; it means being able to disconnect from daily stresses, restore your energy and engage fully with your days. Being well-rested allows the body and mind to recover, fostering a sense of calm and balance.

When you feel rested, you are better equipped to manage stress, maintain focus and approach your daily tasks with clarity and efficiency. Rest helps you stay emotionally balanced, physically strong and ready to tackle the day ahead. In today's busy and fast-paced life, making rest a priority is key to staying energised, improving your mood and being able to handle challenges with calm and confidence.

In this section we discuss the different types of rest, strategies for better sleep and offer some productivity tips so that you can build a balanced rest routine that works for your goals and schedule.

What is rest?

Rest is more than simply stopping - it's an intentional pause that gives your body, mind or emotions space to recover. Scientifically, it refers to a period of reduced physical or mental activity that allows the body to recover, restore energy and return to balance. It can be quiet and still, or gentle and active. It's what helps you feel more grounded, present and able to keep going with care.

Rest and sleep might seem to be the same thing, but they're not. Sleep is a biological need; it is your body's way of shutting down to recharge, repair and reset. It's essential for brain function, memory and overall health. Rest, on the other hand, is about giving yourself a break while you're awake: physically, mentally or emotionally, etc. It could be time spent sitting quietly, stepping away from work or just slowing down to breathe calmly. You can get plenty of sleep and still feel exhausted if you're not giving yourself enough intentional rest throughout the day. Sleep restores your body, but rest restores your energy. You need both to truly feel recharged.

The Seven Types of Rest

According to Dr Saundra Dalton-Smith (author of *Sacred Rest: Recover Your Life, Renew Your Energy, Restore Your Sanity*) [1], rest comes in seven different forms, each playing a key role in helping you recharge and feel your best. Taking care of all seven types of rest can boost your wellbeing, prevent burnout and give you the energy you need to fully enjoy life. When you understand what kind of rest you're missing, you can start making small changes to restore balance, reduce stress and feel more refreshed every day.

THE SEVEN DIFFERENT TYPES OF REST ARE:

- Physical rest.
- Mental rest.
- Sensory rest.
- Creative rest.
- Emotional rest.
- Social rest.
- Spiritual rest.

Self-care ideas for rest

In this chapter, we'll gently explore self-care ideas that support each type of rest. Each one offers a different way to restore your energy – whether you need stillness, creativity, quiet, or connection. You can find small, meaningful ways to care for yourself that fit what you're really needing.

Physical rest

Physical rest is all about giving your body the chance to recover and recharge. It includes both active rest, like gentle stretching, yoga or a leisurely walk; and passive rest, like napping, sitting quietly or simply lying down. By giving your body this time to restore your energy and strength, you set yourself up to feel more refreshed and resilient.

Goal: To help the body recover from physical fatigue and stress.

SELF-CARE IDEAS FOR PHYSICAL REST

GENTLE YOGA Try a restorative yoga class or at-home flow to stretch and relax without exhaustion.

AROMATHERAPY BATH Soak in a warm bath with a few drops of essential oils like lavender, eucalyptus or chamomile to soothe muscles and calm the body.

RESTORATIVE WALKS Go for a slow walk in nature, allowing yourself to fully relax and observe your surroundings.

ACTIVE MUSCLE RECOVERY Spend a few minutes each day doing deep stretches or using a foam roller to relieve muscle tension.

Mental rest

Mental rest means giving your mind time to relax and recharge. It can mean stepping away from distractions, taking a moment to breathe or letting go of all your overwhelming thoughts. It's not about shutting off completely, it's about creating space in your head for clarity and focus. By giving your mind the time that it needs to unwind, you set yourself up to feel calmer, more refreshed and ready to take on the day with a clear head.

Goal: To give the mind a break from constant thinking, planning and mental tasks.

SELF-CARE IDEAS FOR MENTAL REST

COGNITIVE RECHARGE   Use apps like Headspace or Calm to help you clear your mind for a few minutes each day.

FREE PAGES   Write freely in a journal, expressing your thoughts, dreams or just random ideas without any expectations.

COLOURING OR DOODLING   Use adult colouring books or simply doodle to let your mind relax and engage in a creative, non-demanding activity.

DIGITAL DETOX   Take a break from all electronic devices for a few hours – or even an entire day – to give your mind space to decompress.

Sensory rest

Sensory rest is all about giving your senses a break from constant stimulation. It can mean stepping away from screens, dimming the lights or finding a quiet space to escape from noise. The focus can be set on creating moments of calm to let your senses recover and recharge. By giving yourself this time you'll feel more grounded, less overwhelmed and ready to engage with your surroundings in a more balanced way.

Goal: To give your senses a break from overstimulation, such as bright lights or loud noises.

SELF-CARE IDEAS FOR SENSORY REST

DARK ROOM MEDITATION Find a quiet, dark space, sit comfortably, then focus on your breathing or sensations, allowing your senses to take a break from external stimuli.

EYE REST SESSION Lie down with a soft blindfold or eye mask on and relax in a quiet environment to reduce sensory input.

SOOTHING MUSIC OR NATURE SOUNDS Listen to calming music, ocean waves or rainfall to gently stimulate your senses without overwhelming them.

AROMATHERAPY Use calming scents like lavender or sandalwood to help you to draw your focus to your sense of smell and create a peaceful environment.

Creative rest

Creative rest is all about giving your mind the space to recharge and find inspiration again. It's what can happen when you step away from constant problem-solving or brainstorming and instead allow yourself time to soak up things that spark joy – like nature, art, music or even quiet moments. It's not about doing nothing, it's about giving your creativity space to breathe so that new ideas can come to you naturally.

Goal: To refresh and rejuvenate your creative energy.

SELF-CARE IDEAS FOR CREATIVE REST

CREATIVE WRITING   Free-write a poem or short story, or simply write about your day to express your creativity without any pressure for perfection.

PHOTOGRAPHY WALK   Take your camera (or phone) and go for a walk, capturing interesting patterns, textures or moments in nature to inspire your creative side.

MINDFUL CRAFTING   Engage in a relaxing, hands-on project like knitting, pottery or scrapbooking, focusing on the process rather than the outcome.

DIY HOME DECOR   Create simple DIY projects for your home, like decorating a vase, making candles or arranging flowers, to give your creativity room to flow.

Emotional rest

Emotional rest focuses on giving yourself the space to process and release your feelings without too much judgement or pressure. It can mean expressing your emotions more honestly, leaning on a trusted friend or simply allowing yourself to feel things instead of trying to fix everything. Emotional rest is really about creating a safe space for your emotions, in order to let them flow. By taking this time, you'll feel lighter, more balanced and better equipped to handle the ups and downs of life.

Goal: To release emotional stress and recharge emotionally.

SELF-CARE IDEAS FOR EMOTIONAL REST

TALK TO A FRIEND Spend time with a trusted friend or family member and express how you're feeling – whether that's joy, stress or uncertainty.

CRY IT OUT Give yourself permission to cry if you need to, whether through watching a touching movie, listening to an emotional song or simply sitting alone in a comfortable space.

GENTLE REFLECTION Practise daily affirmations or self-compassion exercises, such as repeating kind statements to yourself or looking in the mirror and affirming your worth.

CREATIVE HEALING Create an emotion-based artwork, whether it's an abstract painting, a drawing or a collage, to express and release pent-up emotions.

Social rest

Social rest is about finding balance in your relationships by stepping back from draining interactions and surrounding yourself with supportive, energising people. It can mean taking time for solitude, setting boundaries, or spending quality moments with those who truly uplift you. It's not about isolating yourself; it's about prioritising connections that replenish your energy. By giving yourself this time, you'll feel more refreshed, supported and ready to engage meaningfully with others.

Goal: To recharge by taking a break from social interactions that may feel draining.

SELF-CARE IDEAS FOR SOCIAL REST

SOLO DATE Take yourself out to your favourite café, museum or park, and spend time enjoying your own company and relaxing without the need to socialise.

DISCONNECT FROM SOCIAL MEDIA Take a break from all social media for a day or a week to reduce digital stress and give yourself some quiet time.

READ ALONE Enjoy a good book or listen to an audiobook in a quiet space, allowing yourself to immerse in a world of fiction or new knowledge without outside interaction.

SILENT PAUSE Attend a silent retreat or practise a period of silence (even just a day) to reset your social energy.

Spiritual rest

Spiritual rest centres around reconnecting with a deeper sense of meaning, purpose or connection beyond the everyday. It can mean spending time in prayer, meditation or nature, or simply reflecting on what truly matters to you. It's not about following any set path – it's about nurturing your inner self and finding moments of peace and grounding. By giving yourself this time, you'll feel more aligned, fulfilled and connected to something greater than yourself.

Goal: To reconnect with your sense of purpose, values and inner peace.

SELF-CARE IDEAS FOR SPIRITUAL REST

EARTH CONNECTION WALK Take a walk through a natural setting and reflect on the beauty and interconnectedness of the world.

PRAYER OR AFFIRMATIONS Spend time in prayer or recite affirmations that align with your spiritual beliefs, helping you to centre your thoughts and connect with a higher power.

VOLUNTEER Give back to your community or a cause you believe in, fostering a sense of fulfilment and spiritual alignment through service.

NATURE IMMERSION Spend time outdoors – whether it's hiking in the mountains, sitting by a river or meditating in a garden – to experience a sense of awe and spiritual connection with nature.

Overcoming guilt

It's easy to feel guilty about taking time to rest, especially in a world that values constant productivity. But resting isn't laziness – it's essential. When you give yourself permission to pause, you're not slacking off; you're recharging your energy and protecting your wellbeing. Remember, you can't pour from an empty cup. Taking time to rest makes you stronger, sharper and more present for the things and people that matter. Rest isn't something you have to earn – it's something you deserve.

A letter to rest

Use these prompts to guide you through this reflective journaling exercise on rest.

WHAT ARE THE BEST THINGS THAT REST HAS GIVEN YOU? WRITE ABOUT SPECIFIC MOMENTS WHEN REST HELPED YOU FEEL RECHARGED, HAPPY OR AT PEACE.

....

....

WHAT MAKES YOU HESITATE TO FULLY EMBRACE REST? EXPLORE ANY FEELINGS OF GUILT, FRUSTRATION OR RESISTANCE TOWARDS IT.

....

....

IF YOU COULD CREATE AN IDEAL RELATIONSHIP WITH REST, WHAT WOULD IT LOOK LIKE?

....

....

....

....

WRITE ABOUT THE BOUNDARIES YOU'D SET TO PROTECT YOUR REST TIME IN THE FUTURE.

....

....

....

....

Dealing with productivity pressure

Have you ever felt like your worth depends on how much you get done in a day? It's a common feeling – tying productivity to self-worth – but it can create an exhausting cycle. Suddenly, rest feels like 'wasted time', and your value seems measured by how much you accomplish. The truth is, your worth isn't about how productive you are – it's simply part of who you are. Shifting your mindset from 'I am what I achieve' to 'I am valuable because I exist' can help you build a healthier relationship with both productivity and self-care. Productivity should be a tool to support growth, not a ruler to measure your value. When we push ourselves relentlessly without breaks, it can take a toll on our mental health, leading to burnout, stress and anxiety. Remember, rest and self-care aren't luxuries – they're necessities.

Dealing with burnout

Burnout is a deep, overwhelming exhaustion that goes beyond just feeling tired; it's a kind of physical, mental and emotional depletion all at once. It happens when stress and pressure build up over time, when you've not had enough rest or balance, leaving you more drained, unmotivated and disconnected. Simple tasks often feel impossible, focus disappears, and even things you once loved start to feel like a burden. You may feel irritable, numb or emotionally distant, struggling to find enough energy to care. Burnout can also take a toll on your body, causing headaches, trouble sleeping, weakened immune system and constant fatigue. It's a signal that something needs to change – whether it's just slowing down, setting boundaries or prioritising real time to rest and recover.

Below are some prompts to help reframe your relationship with rest. Use these as your reminder to prioritise time to rest. Even better, why not try adding in a few of your own?

REST	BETTER SELF-TALK
Rest is unproductive.	Rest is a powerful way to recharge so I can show up fully when I need to.
I don't deserve rest if I haven't finished everything on my to-do list.	Rest is not something I have to earn – it's something I need and deserve every day.
If I slow down, I'll fall behind.	When I allow myself to slow down, I come back stronger and more focused.
Rest is for later, after I've achieved my goals.	Rest is part of the process that helps me achieve my goals.

REST	BETTER SELF-TALK
Pushing through exhaustion is the only way to succeed.	Listening to my body and resting when needed is key to sustaining my success.
People will think I'm weak if I take time for myself.	Prioritising rest shows strength and self-awareness, not weakness.

How can we combat burnout?

What science tells us ...

1. EXERCISE CAN CUT THE RISK OF BURNOUT

Regular physical exercise has been shown to reduce the risk of burnout by helping to relieve stress and improve mood [2].

2. TAKING BREAKS CAN DECREASE YOUR FATIGUE

Taking breaks during your working day can alleviate stress and enhance focus. For instance, a study found that brief, frequent micro-breaks can reduce stress and significantly decrease fatigue. Longer breaks were found to provide greater improvements in performance [3].

3. SETTING BOUNDARIES CAN SUPPORT YOUR WELLBEING

People who set clear boundaries around work, such as limiting after-hours emails or refusing extra tasks, report lower levels of burnout. Setting and maintaining boundaries is an important way to support wellbeing and prevent burnout [4].

Your rest routine

Instead of waiting until the point of overwhelm to stop, you can create pockets of rest throughout your day – small but meaningful moments to reset. These don't have to be big or time-consuming; even taking a few deep breaths, a quiet moment or stepping away from a screen can help. Prioritising rest daily, in ways that meet your specific needs, ensures that you're not just pushing through exhaustion but actively refuelling your energy as you go.

By integrating different types of rest into your routine – whether it's mental rest through a midday pause, sensory rest by reducing screen time or emotional rest through journaling or talking to a friend, you create a balanced approach that keeps you feeling refreshed, present and engaged every day.

Realistic rest routine

What if incorporating some rest into your day could take only a few minutes? Here's how to make rest a habit, no matter how busy life gets:

- 💚 **Physical rest** Stretch, take deep breaths or simply sit still for a moment.

- 💚 **Mental rest** Give your brain a break by stepping away from screens or switching tasks.

- 💚 **Emotional rest** Talk to someone you trust or write down your thoughts to process emotions.

- 💚 **Social rest** Spend time alone if you need to recharge, or surround yourself with uplifting people.

- 💚 **Sensory rest** Reduce noise, dim the lights or take a break from your phone.

- 💚 **Creative rest** Get inspired by nature or music, or simply let your mind wander.

- 💚 **Spiritual rest** Take five minutes to reflect, meditate, pray or reconnect with yourself.

Even small moments of rest add up – pausing for a few deep breaths, stepping outside for fresh air or giving yourself permission to slow down can make all the difference. Rest isn't a reward, it's a necessity – and when you make it a daily priority, everything else in life feels more manageable.

Your self-care for rest library

	SELF-CARE ACTIVITIES	NOTES
PHYSICAL REST	Gentle yoga	
	Aromatherapy bath	
	Restorative walks	
	Active muscle recovery	
MENTAL REST	Cognitive recharge	
	Free pages	
	Colouring or doodling	
	Digital detox	

	SELF-CARE ACTIVITIES	NOTES
SENSORY REST	Dark room meditation	
SENSORY REST	Eye rest session	
SENSORY REST	Soothing music or nature sounds	
SENSORY REST	Aromatherapy	
EMOTIONAL REST	Talking to a friend	
EMOTIONAL REST	Crying it out	
EMOTIONAL REST	Self-compassion rituals	
EMOTIONAL REST	Creative healing	
SOCIAL REST	Solo date	
SOCIAL REST	Disconnecting from social media	
SOCIAL REST	Reading alone	
SOCIAL REST	Silent pause	
SPIRITUAL REST	Earth connection walk	
SPIRITUAL REST	Prayer or affirmations	
SPIRITUAL REST	Volunteering	
SPIRITUAL REST	Nature immersion	

PART 3

feeling mindful

Feeling mindful refers to a state of mind-body presence, where one is fully engaged in the current moment with acceptance and non-judgement. This means being aware of your thoughts, emotions and sensations without being overwhelmed by them, fostering a sense of clarity and peace.

When feeling mindful, you are more capable of managing stress, responding thoughtfully rather than reacting impulsively, and nurturing meaningful connections with others. Mindfulness improves emotional balance, sharpens focus and cultivates a deeper appreciation for the present. In a busy and distracting world, mindfulness helps you stay grounded, making it easier to handle life with calm and focus.

In this section, we delve into self-care ideas for cultivating presence, how to break free from autopilot habits and practical strategies to create an intentional mindfulness routine that helps you feel calm.

EVERY TIMELINE IS VALID:

- ♥ Graduating at 35 is still an honour.
- ♥ Starting a new career at 40 is still a fresh start.
- ♥ Finding your passion at 50 is still meaningful.

- ♥ Falling in love at 60 is still beautiful.
- ♥ Healing at 70 is still growth.
- ♥ Learning a new skill at any age is still progress.
- ♥ Changing paths when it feels right is still courageous.

What is mindfulness?

Mindfulness isn't about clearing your mind or achieving some perfect state of calm. It's simply about being present – whether that's noticing the warmth of the sun on your skin, truly listening to a friend or taking a deep breath when life feels overwhelming. By practising mindfulness, you give yourself space to breathe, think and reconnect with what really matters.

KEY COMPONENTS OF MINDFULNESS

- ♥ **BEING PRESENT** Fully experiencing the moment without distraction.

- ♥ **NON-JUDGEMENTAL ACCEPTANCE** Not labelling thoughts or feelings as good or bad, just observing them.

- ♥ **FOCUSED ATTENTION** Training your mind to concentrate on one thing at a time, like your breath or surroundings.

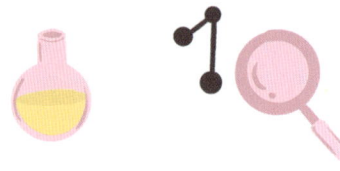

Should you give mindfulness practice a try?

What science tells us ...

1. MINDFULNESS CAN REDUCE YOUR STRESS LEVELS AND KEEP YOU ALERT

Studies show that a short mindfulness session can help you feel less stressed, but it might also boost your body's cortisol response to social pressure. This could mean that mindfulness encourages active coping, making stress feel more manageable while keeping your body alert and ready to respond. [6]

2. YOU CAN SLEEP BETTER AND FEEL RESTED WITH MINDFULNESS

A simple, community-based mindfulness programme helped older adults sleep better than a highly structured sleep education course. Not only did it improve sleep quality, it also reduced daytime tiredness, making a real difference in daily life and overall wellbeing. [7]

3. STARTING YOUR PRACTICE WITH ONLINE RESOURCES AND APPS IS JUST AS EFFECTIVE!

Mindfulness meditation works even when practised online! Studies show that internet-based mindfulness programmes can reduce anxiety, depression and insomnia, offering a promising (and more accessible!) alternative to traditional treatment. [5]

Living on autopilot mode

Have you ever caught yourself going through the motions of your day without really noticing what's happening around you? When you're on autopilot, life can start to feel like a blur – you go through the motions without really thinking or feeling present. Small moments of joy can pass you by, and decisions might become automatic rather than intentional. Over time, this can lead to feeling more disconnected from yourself and others, increased stress and even burnout. You might find yourself stuck in routines that don't actually serve you, making choices out of habit rather than what truly benefits you. Being on autopilot can also affect your mental wellbeing, leaving you feeling emotionally drained or like you're 'going through the motions' rather than actively living.

Leaving autopilot mode

The first step you can take if you find yourself living on autopilot is to start paying attention – notice the small moments in your day instead of rushing through them. Pause and check in with yourself – how are you feeling? What do you actually want right now? Switch up your routine – take a different route to work, try a new hobby or eat somewhere different. Be present when talking to others – really listen, instead of just waiting for your turn to speak. Slow down and do one thing at a time – whether it's drinking your coffee, walking outside or even just breathing. The more you bring awareness to your daily life, the more you'll feel engaged, intentional and alive.

Bringing mindfulness into your daily life helps you break free from autopilot by encouraging you to slow down, pay attention and fully experience each moment with intention and awareness.

SELF-CHECK-IN EXERCISE:
Are you living on autopilot?

DO YOU GO THROUGH YOUR DAY WITHOUT REALLY THINKING ABOUT WHAT YOU'RE DOING?

....

....

CAN YOU REMEMBER WHAT YOU HAD FOR BREAKFAST (OR ANOTHER RECENT MEAL) WITHOUT EFFORT?

....

....

DO YOU OFTEN REACH THE END OF THE DAY AND WONDER WHERE THE TIME WENT?

....

....

HAVE YOU CAUGHT YOURSELF ARRIVING AT A DESTINATION WITHOUT REMEMBERING THE JOURNEY?

....

....

ARE YOU FREQUENTLY OVERWHELMED BUT UNSURE WHY?

....

....

Self-care for mindfulness

In your daily routine you can incorporate simple practices and habits to cultivate mindfulness. Mindfulness is a state of being fully present in both mind and body, which requires conscious awareness and engagement in the moment. While this may seem challenging at times, self-care activities can help you develop this state of presence. One way to approach mindfulness is by exploring practices that nurture the body, mind and soul, creating a well-rounded and intentional way to stay grounded in daily life.

Why divide mindfulness into mind, body and soul rather than treating it as a single practice?

This approach was chosen to highlight the different dimensions of mindfulness: the body, the mind and a deeper sense of connection – so you can explore mindfulness in a way that feels most relevant to you. By breaking it down into mindfulness for the body, mind and soul, this structure helps you focus on what you need most at any given time.

- 💜 If you're feeling physically tense, body-based mindfulness can help you release stress through movement and awareness.

- 💜 If your mind feels cluttered, mental mindfulness can bring clarity and focus.

- 💜 If you're seeking a deeper sense of balance or emotional wellbeing, soulful mindfulness offers a way to reconnect.

Of course, mindfulness doesn't always fit neatly into categories – many practices overlap, and 'mindfulness for the soul' may mean different things to different people. But rather than overcomplicating mindfulness, use the self-care activities discussed here as a simple, flexible way to integrate it into daily life in a way that works for you.

For the body

Mindful self-care for the body is all about tuning in to physical sensations, movement and relaxation with full awareness. Instead of just going through the motions, these practices help you connect with your body in a gentle, intentional way.

Body scan meditation

A body scan meditation is often the first step in mindfulness meditation, which involves bringing awareness to different parts of your body. This practice can be easily incorporated into your daily routine, whether you are sitting on a train during your commute or lying in bed before sleep.

Take four simple steps to get started

- **GET COMFORTABLE** Sit or lie down in a relaxed position.

- **SCAN YOUR BODY** Close your eyes and slowly bring awareness to different parts of your body, noticing any tension or sensations.

- **FEEL THE CONNECTION** Pay attention to where your body makes contact with the chair, bed or floor, and notice any warmth, tingling or tightness as you move your awareness from your toes upwards.

- **FOCUS ON YOUR BREATH** Shift your awareness to your breathing, observing the natural rhythm of air moving in and out of your body.

Tip: Engage in this exercise for a few minutes, then pause and ask yourself:

- 💜 How does my body feel right now?
- 💜 Where am I holding tension?
- 💜 What sensations am I noticing that I usually overlook?

This practice helps ground you in the present moment, promoting relaxation, self-awareness and stress relief.

Mindful stretching

Mindful stretching is a simple way to bring awareness to your body while releasing tension. Instead of rushing through the movements, focus on how your muscles feel as you stretch. You can incorporate this practice at any time of the day.

Creative ways to practise this exercise

- **STRETCH IN NATURE** Practise stretching outside and feel the fresh air as you move.

- **MOVE TO MUSIC** Play soft, calming music and let your body flow with the rhythm.

- **MORNING WAKE-UP STRETCH** Start your day by stretching in bed before getting up.

- **DESK STRETCHING** Release tension by stretching while sitting at your desk.

- **WIND-DOWN ROUTINE** Use gentle stretching before bed to help your body relax.

These ideas make stretching feel more natural and enjoyable in everyday life!

Tip: As you stretch, notice any tension, stiffness or areas that need extra care. Ask yourself:

- 💜 Which parts of my body feel the most tense?
- 💜 How does my breathing change as I stretch?
- 💜 What movements feel the most releasing for me?

Taking a few minutes for mindful stretching can help you feel more present, more relaxed and connected to your body.

Walking meditation

A walking meditation is a simple way to bring mindfulness into your daily routine. Instead of walking on autopilot, this practice encourages you to slow down and focus on each step with intention. The goal is to connect with the rhythm of your movement and the sensation of your feet touching the ground.

Three simple ways to practise walking meditation

♥ **SET THE SCENE**   Choose a quiet place where you can walk without distractions, whether it's a peaceful outdoor path or a clear space indoors. Before starting, pause for a moment, take a deep breath and bring awareness to your posture.

♥ **MOVE WITH INTENTION**   Walk slowly, paying attention to the way your feet touch the ground – heel first, then the ball of your foot, then your toes. Sync your breathing with each step, inhaling as you lift your foot and exhaling as you place it down.

STAY PRESENT If your mind starts to wander, gently bring your focus back to the rhythm of your steps and the sensations in your body. Let each step be a reminder to stay grounded and fully in the moment.

Tip: Try to engage all your senses during the walk. Ask yourself:

 What textures do I feel beneath my feet?

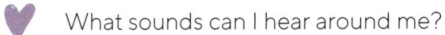 What sounds can I hear around me?

How does my body feel as I move?

A walking meditation helps you slow down, clear your mind and feel more present in your surroundings. Even a few minutes of mindful walking can bring a sense of calm and clarity to your day.

For the mind

Mindfulness for the mind is about bringing awareness to your thoughts, focus and emotions, helping you create mental clarity and ease rather than getting lost in distractions or overthinking.

Breath awareness

Breath awareness is a simple yet powerful way to ground yourself in the present moment. By focusing on your breath you can calm your mind, reduce stress and create a sense of balance in your body. This practice can be done anywhere and there are plenty of guided breathing exercises available for free that can help you stay on track!

BREATHE IN, BREATHE OUT – A SIMPLE GUIDE

- Sit or lie down in a comfortable position, relax your shoulders and close your eyes, if it feels natural.

- Take a slow breath in through your nose, filling your belly with air, then exhale gently through your mouth, releasing any tension.

- Focus on the rhythm of your breath – how it moves in and out, the rise and fall of your body and the temperature of the air.

- If your mind wanders, gently bring your attention back to your breath, using it as an anchor to the present moment.

Tip: Try this exercise for a few minutes and notice how you feel. Ask yourself:

- Is my breathing shallow or deep?

- How does my body respond when I focus on my breath?

- Do I feel calmer, more focused or more present after this exercise?

Single-tasking

Single-tasking is the practice of giving your full attention to one thing at a time. In a world that constantly encourages multi-tasking, this simple shift can help you feel more focused, less overwhelmed and more present in your daily life.

Simple ideas for single-tasking

- 💜 **LISTEN FULLY** Give your full attention to music, a podcast or a conversation without multi-tasking.

- 💜 **ENJOY YOUR MORNING DRINK** Pause to appreciate the warmth, aroma and taste of your coffee or tea.

- 💜 **READ UNDISTURBED** Silence your phone and immerse yourself in a book without distractions.

- 💜 **FOCUS COMPLETELY** If you engage in a hobby such as drawing, baking or crafting, allow yourself to complete this activity without interruptions.

Tip: Pay attention to how single-tasking feels compared to multi-tasking. Ask yourself:

💜 Do I feel more present and engaged?

💜 Is my mind less scattered when I focus on just one thing?

💜 How does slowing down change the way I experience simple activities?

By practising single-tasking, you can bring more clarity, focus and enjoyment to everyday moments – one task at a time.

Five senses check-in

A five senses check-in is a simple grounding exercise that helps bring you back to the present moment by tuning into what you can see, hear, touch, smell and taste. This exercise is an easy way to practise that, helping to reduce stress, improve focus and create a sense of calm wherever you are.

How to get started with the five senses check-in exercise

- ♥ **SEE** Name five things around you, noticing small details like shadows or colours.

- ♥ **HEAR** Close your eyes and list four sounds, from loud noises to subtle background hums.

- ♥ **TOUCH** Focus on three sensations, like fabric texture, warmth or the surface beneath you.

- ♥ **SMELL** Identify two scents, whether strong like coffee or faint like fresh air.

TASTE Notice one flavour, either from food, drink or the lingering taste in your mouth.

Tip: Try this check-in whenever you feel overwhelmed, distracted or disconnected. Ask yourself:

 Do I feel more present after tuning into my senses?

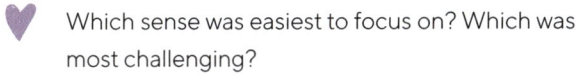 Which sense was easiest to focus on? Which was most challenging?

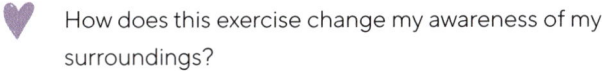 How does this exercise change my awareness of my surroundings?

By regularly practising a five senses check-in, you can bring yourself back to the present moment, one sensation at a time.

For the soul

Mindfulness for the soul is about nurturing a sense of connection – whether to yourself, others or something greater – allowing you to find more meaning, peace and inner balance.

Gratitude pause

A gratitude pause is a simple yet powerful way to shift your focus to the positive aspects of your life. This exercise takes only a few moments but can make a meaningful difference to how you feel.

A SIMPLE GUIDE TO A GRATITUDE PAUSE

- Take a deep breath and bring your awareness to the present moment.
- Think of three things you're grateful for – they can be big or small, from a supportive friend to a warm cup of tea.
- Say them out loud or write them down, fully appreciating each one.
- Pause for a moment to reflect on how these things add joy, comfort or meaning to your life.

Tip: Try this practice daily – morning, night or whenever you need a boost. Ask yourself:

- How does expressing gratitude shift my mindset?
- Did I notice something today that I might usually take for granted?
- How does gratitude feel in my body?

By taking a quick pause for gratitude, you can bring more joy and appreciation into your everyday life.

Journaling your feelings

Journaling is a simple and effective way to process emotions, reduce stress and gain clarity. The key is to write freely, without feeling judgement or pressure to make it perfect.

PRACTICAL TIPS TO JOURNAL YOUR FEELINGS

- Find a quiet space and grab a notebook or open a blank document.

- Start writing without overthinking. Let your emotions flow onto the page, whether they are clear or messy.

- Notice what comes up. If you're unsure where to start, write about what's on your mind or how you feel in this moment.

- Keep going for a few minutes, without worrying about grammar or structure. Just let the words take shape naturally.

Tip: If you need guidance, try prompts like:

♥ What emotions am I feeling right now?

♥ What's been weighing on my mind lately?

♥ What's something I need to let go of?

Journaling helps you release bottled-up thoughts, gain self-awareness and create space for emotional clarity.

Loving-kindness meditation

Loving-kindness meditation is a mindfulness practice that cultivates compassion, connection and inner peace; this practice originates from ancient Buddhist traditions and it has been widely studied in modern-day research.

LOVING-KINDNESS MEDITATION STEP-BY-STEP

- Close your eyes and take a deep breath, relaxing into the moment.

- Silently repeat kind phrases to yourself, such as:

'May I be happy. May I be peaceful. May I be healthy. May I be free from suffering.'

- Expand this kindness to others – think of a loved one, a friend, a stranger, or even someone you find challenging. Wish them the same wellbeing:

'May you be happy. May you be peaceful. May you be free from suffering.'

 Take a moment to sit with these feelings of warmth and compassion before gently opening your eyes.

Tip: Try this practice whenever you feel stressed, disconnected or in need of emotional balance. Ask yourself:

 How does it feel to direct kindness towards myself?

 Was it easier or harder to send kindness to others?

 How does this shift my perspective on relationships and emotions?

By practising loving-kindness meditation you can create space to nurture self-compassion, emotional resilience and a greater sense of connection to the world around you.

Your mindfulness routine

Instead of rushing through the day on autopilot, you can create small moments of mindfulness; simple pauses that help you feel more present and balanced. These don't have to take up much time; even a few deep, intentional breaths can anchor you in the moment, allowing you to reset.

Mindfulness isn't about doing more – it's about doing things with awareness. Whether it's starting your morning with breath awareness, enjoying a meal without distractions or taking a moment to step outside and notice your surroundings, small acts of slow living can help you reconnect with yourself. Prioritising these moments throughout the day ensures you're not just getting through life, but actually experiencing it with clarity and calm.

Realistic mindful moments

Mindfulness doesn't have to be time-consuming – small, intentional moments throughout the day can help you feel more present and grounded. Here are a few simple ways to bring mindfulness into your routine, no matter how busy you are:

- 💜 Take one deep, intentional breath.
- 💜 Sip your drink slowly and notice the taste.
- 💜 Put your phone down for 30 seconds and just be.
- 💜 Feel your feet on the ground as you walk.
- 💜 Close your eyes and listen to surrounding sounds.
- 💜 Stretch and notice how your body feels.
- 💜 Chew your food slowly and taste each bite.
- 💜 Look out the window and observe one small detail.
- 💜 Rub your hands together and feel the warmth.
- 💜 Blink slowly and relax your face for a moment.

Your self-care for mindfulness library

	SELF-CARE ACTIVITIES	NOTES
MINDFULNESS FOR YOUR BODY	Body scan meditation	
	Mindful stretching	
	Walking meditation	

	SELF-CARE ACTIVITIES	NOTES
MINDFULNESS FOR YOUR MIND	Breath awareness	
	Single-tasking	
	Five senses check-in	
MINDFULNESS FOR YOUR SOUL	Gratitude pause	
	Journaling your feelings	
	Loving-kindness meditation	

PART 4
feeling centred

Feeling centred refers to a state of mental, emotional and physical balance where one feels grounded, focused and in control despite external pressures or internal turmoil. It is the ability to maintain stability and clarity in the face of life's challenges, fostering a sense of calm and resilience.

When feeling centred, you are better equipped to manage stress, make thoughtful decisions and maintain healthy relationships. It helps you manage your emotions, think clearly and feel more connected to yourself and the present moment. In a busy and often overwhelming world, staying centred acts as your anchor, making it easier to handle life's challenges with calm and confidence.

In this section of the book we explore feeling centred, practising self-compassion and creating self-care plans; here you can find the space to build balanced and grounding daily routines that nurture your happiness.

PICK THE AFFIRMATION THAT YOU NEED:

- I own my growth, flaws and all.
- I let go of what doesn't serve me.
- I am stronger than my inner critic.

♥ I choose grace over guilt.

♥ I deserve kindness, especially from myself.

♥ I am allowed to rest and reset.

Self-care ideas for staying centred

Self-compassion is about treating yourself with the same kindness, patience and understanding that you would offer a close friend. Instead of being overly self-critical, it means recognising that mistakes, struggles and imperfections are part of being human. This involves being gentle with yourself, acknowledging difficult emotions without judgement, and reminding yourself that you are worthy of care and kindness – especially in moments of failure or self-doubt. It's not about avoiding responsibility but about approaching challenges with self-support rather than self-criticism, creating space for healing and self-acceptance.

Research shows that self-compassion reduces stress, increases resilience and improves overall wellbeing, making it a powerful tool for emotional balance. Based on the definition originally developed by the researcher Dr Kristin Neff, the concept of self-compassion is often described through three key elements: self-kindness, common humanity and mindfulness [10].

♥ Self-kindness means being gentle with yourself rather than harshly critical, offering warmth and understanding when things don't go as planned.

♥ Common humanity is the reminder that struggles, mistakes and setbacks are part of being human – no one is alone in their challenges.

♥ And mindfulness helps us acknowledge our difficult emotions without suppressing or exaggerating them, allowing us to respond with balance rather than self-judgement.

Together, these elements create a foundation for self-compassion, helping us navigate life with greater resilience, acceptance and care. Let's look at these three components in more depth.

Self-kindness

Self-kindness is about treating yourself with warmth and understanding, especially in difficult moments. Instead of responding with harsh self-criticism, it means offering yourself the same patience and care that you would give to a friend. Life comes with setbacks, mistakes and challenges, but rather than punishing yourself for them, self-kindness encourages you to practise gentleness and encouragement. It's not about ignoring personal growth, it's about creating a supportive space where you can learn and move forward without unnecessary self-blame.

Common humanity

At times, it's easy to feel alone in our struggles, as if no one else could possibly understand what you're going through. Common humanity reminds us that suffering and imperfection are part of being human. Everyone faces difficulties, makes mistakes and experiences moments of doubt. Recognising this can ease feelings of isolation and make it easier to be compassionate towards yourself. Instead of asking, *'Why is this happening to me?'*, self-compassion can shift the perspective to *'This is part of life, and I am not alone in this.'*

Balanced awareness

Originally called mindfulness, the balanced awareness component of self-compassion is about being present with your emotions – acknowledging them without suppressing or exaggerating them. Rather than getting lost in self-judgement or avoidance, mindfulness allows you to observe your thoughts and feelings with balance and acceptance. This means noticing pain or discomfort without letting it define you. When practised alongside self-kindness and common humanity, mindfulness creates the foundation for self-compassion, helping you respond to challenges with clarity, care and a sense of perspective.

Can self-compassion really make a difference to your life?

What science tells us ...

1. SELF-COMPASSION IS LINKED TO LOWER ANXIETY AND LESSER LOW MOOD

Studies show that people with higher self-compassion tend to experience less anxiety and depression. Kindness to oneself truly is linked to better emotional wellbeing [8].

2. EVEN SHORT SELF-COMPASSION EXERCISES CAN IMPROVE MOOD

Research has found that brief self-compassion exercises can lift your mood, reduce self-criticism and boost warm, connected feelings – offering benefits similar to excitement, but with a gentler, more caring tone [9].

3. SELF-KINDNESS MAY SUPPORT PHYSICAL HEALTH, TOO

One study found that self-compassion can indirectly improve physical health by lowering stress and encouraging healthy behaviours. Taking a kind, accepting and mindful approach to your flaws and challenges may help your body as well as your mind [11].

Practising gratitude

Let's try a mindfulness exercise that brings together different elements of feeling centred.

Gently hold out one hand in front of you. With the index finger of your other hand, touch each finger one by one, pausing to name something you're grateful for in a specific category. Take a slow breath with each one. Let the moment land.

Note: When you catch your mind wandering (because it is normal for this to happen!) kindly and gently bring it back to the exercise.

ONE FINGER AT A TIME

- **THUMB** – Something you tasted.
  A comforting meal, a warm drink, a sweet treat.

- **INDEX FINGER** – Something you smelled.
  Fresh bread, flowers, your favourite soap.

- **MIDDLE FINGER** – Something you saw.
  Sunlight, a smile, your pet, something beautiful.

- **RING FINGER** – Something you heard.
  Laughter, a kind voice, your favourite song.

- **PINKY** – Something you touched.
  A soft blanket, warm mug, your pet's fur.

- 💛 **THUMB (OTHER HAND)** – A person you're grateful for.
  A friend, family member or someone kind.

- 💛 **INDEX FINGER** – A kindness you received.
  A compliment, a helping hand, someone's patience.

- 💛 **MIDDLE FINGER** – A part of yourself you appreciate.
  Your courage, your sense of humour, your heart.

- 💛 **RING FINGER** – Something about today that mattered.
  A small win, a good rest, a moment of peace.

- 💛 **PINKY** – Something you're looking forward to.
  A quiet evening, a favourite meal, a tiny joy ahead.

'Being gentle with yourself is part of growing, not an obstacle to it.'

Your centred self-care routine

SELF-LOVE -> BUILDING BETTER HABITS

Building better habits is like laying stepping stones towards a more grounded version of you. These habits don't need to be big or dramatic; they can be as simple as taking a slow breath, keeping a morning ritual or pausing to notice how you feel. Each small act of consistency becomes an anchor, helping you feel more steady, more present and more in tune with what matters to you. Over time, these habits become your pathway home – to a calm, centred space within.

Next, we'll explore how to gently weave these better habits into your self-care plans and routines – little practices you can apply to your mornings, evenings and throughout your day.

Creating self-care plans

Having a self-care plan you can turn to in specific situations – like busy days, stressful moments or low moods – can be a powerful way to stay grounded and supported when you need it most. These kinds of plans act as gentle guides, helping you respond to life's ups and downs with care instead of overwhelm.

Whether it's a 'tough times plan' filled with comforting rituals, a 'busy day plan' with simple grounding pauses, or a 'night routine plan' focused on rest, knowing you have something in place makes it easier to give yourself what you need. Rather than trying to think of what might help in the moment, you have a list of small, nurturing actions ready – like a toolkit for your wellbeing, created with love in advance.

Start by identifying what you need most in each situation – whether it's more rest, emotional support, focus, connection or a sense of calm. Choose simple, realistic practices that fit into your routine, like drinking water in the morning, journaling for a few minutes at

night, taking a screen-free pause or repeating a calming affirmation. The key is to keep it flexible and kind – your plan should feel supportive, not overwhelming.

Check in with yourself regularly to see what's helping, what isn't and what you might want to try next. Over time, these small moments of care can add up to something truly grounding and nourishing.

Your morning routine

A morning routine creates a gentle and intentional start to the day, helping to shift from rest into focus with ease. Small habits like stretching, hydrating or spending a quiet moment with a cup of tea or coffee can support both physical energy and emotional balance. With consistency, a morning routine becomes a way to ground the day in calm, clarity and purpose – no matter what follows.

A morning routine doesn't need to be long – just 10 minutes can make a meaningful difference. Starting the day with a few deep breaths or gentle stretches helps wake up the body. Drinking a glass of water and enjoying a warm drink mindfully can boost energy and focus. Writing down a simple to-do list or a short journal entry can help set intentions for the day ahead. Even taking a quiet moment by a window or stepping outside for fresh air can offer clarity. In just a few minutes, these small acts create a sense of calm, purpose and readiness for whatever the day brings.

Tiny habits for your morning routine

 MAKE A SHORT LIST OF THINGS THAT HELP YOU FEEL GROUNDED IN THE MORNING.

This could be anything from sipping tea slowly to stepping outside for fresh air – simple rituals that make mornings feel gentler.

 SET A GENTLE ALARM THAT DOESN'T JOLT YOU AWAKE.

Choose a sound or song that feels calm and welcoming to help you start the day without stress.

 SPEND 10 MINUTES DOING SMALL THINGS THAT SET THE TONE FOR THE DAY.

Make your bed, open the window, stretch or write a quick to-do list to create a sense of calm and focus.

CHECK IN WITH YOURSELF BEFORE CHECKING IN WITH THE WORLD.

Notice how you're feeling, physically and emotionally, before picking up your phone or diving into tasks.

ENERGISE YOUR BODY WITH MOVEMENT OR BREATH.

Do a few stretches, breathe deeply or go for a short walk to gently wake up your body.

NOURISH YOUR MIND WITH SOMETHING UPLIFTING.

Read a short passage, listen to calming music or reflect on an intention for the day ahead.

START YOUR DAY WITH A SIMPLE AFFIRMATION.

Try something like: 'I am ready for today. I can move at my own pace. This day is mine.'

Your morning self-care plan

A morning self-care plan isn't about ticking off tasks, it's a chance to start your day with calm and intention. It's a gentle moment to wake up your body, clear your mind and set a kind tone for the day ahead. Find some inspiration below for some realistic morning activities based on how much time you have at your disposal.

FIVE-MINUTE MORNING SELF-CARE IDEAS	TEN-MINUTE MORNING SELF-CARE IDEAS	ONE-HOUR MORNING SELF-CARE IDEAS
Drink a glass of water with lemon to rehydrate.	Prepare and enjoy your favourite tea or coffee slowly.	Take a nature walk or light jog in the morning sun.

FIVE-MINUTE MORNING SELF-CARE IDEAS	TEN-MINUTE MORNING SELF-CARE IDEAS	ONE-HOUR MORNING SELF-CARE IDEAS
Write down one thing you're grateful for.	Take a mindful shower, focusing on its warmth and scent.	Do a full-body yoga or movement session.
Repeat a morning affirmation or intention aloud.	Tidy your space - make your bed or clear a small surface.	Plan your day with care, including breaks and things that bring you joy.
Step outside for a few deep breaths of fresh air.	Do a short guided meditation or breathwork session.	Enjoy a slow, nourishing breakfast without distractions.
Do a gentle neck and shoulders stretch.	Journal three things you're looking forward to today.	Read or listen to a podcast that inspires or calms you.

Use this space to help you create a centring ritual that works for you by listing five practices you want to try (if this feels overwhelming, you can start with just one tomorrow!):

PRACTICE 1

....

....

....

....

PRACTICE 2

....

....

....

....

PRACTICE 3

....
....
....
....

PRACTICE 4

....
....
....

PRACTICE 5

....
....
....

Self-care plan for busy days

A self-care plan for busy days is all about creating small pockets of calm that help you move through a full schedule without losing yourself in the rush. Prepping ahead – like setting out clothes, cooking meals or writing a simple to-do list the night before – can ease the pressure first thing in the morning. Starting your day by 'eating the frog' (tackling the hardest task first) clears mental space and builds momentum.
Throughout the day, weaving in quick sensory resets – like stepping outside for fresh air, splashing cool water on your face or listening to calming music – can help ground you when everything feels fast. Keeping a water bottle nearby, scheduling short movement or breathing breaks and giving yourself permission to pause, even for just a minute, helps you stay connected to yourself. On busy days, the goal isn't to do everything perfectly, it's to move through the day with small acts of care that support your energy, focus and calm.

Tiny habits to prep for busy days

SET OUT WHAT YOU'LL NEED FOR THE MORNING THE NIGHT BEFORE.

Lay out your clothes, pack your bag or prep breakfast – these small choices will make things run smoother later.

MAKE A SHORT LIST OF YOUR TOP THREE PRIORITIES.

Focus on what truly needs your attention so you can move into the day with more clarity and less stress.

DO A LIGHT TIDY OF YOUR SPACE.

Clear surfaces or put things in place – waking up to a calm environment can help you feel more in control.

FILL YOUR WATER BOTTLE AND PREPARE ANY SNACKS.

Having something ready to nourish you during the day saves time and helps you stay grounded.

CHOOSE A GENTLE WIND-DOWN TIME.

Decide when you'll switch off screens or begin your evening routine to protect your energy for the next day.

ADD SOMETHING KIND TO LOOK FORWARD TO.

Even on the busiest days, a moment of joy – a cup of your favourite tea, a comforting scent or a cosy five-minute break – can make all the difference.

Your busy days' self-care plan

Even on the busiest days, there's space for care. This plan isn't about adding more to your list – it's about protecting small, meaningful habits that help you stay grounded, even when things are full. Think of these moments as anchors that support you through the rush.

TIME OF DAY	TINY HABITS THAT SUPPORTED ME	HOW IT HELPS ME FEEL
MORNING		
MIDDAY		

TIME OF DAY	TINY HABITS THAT SUPPORTED ME	HOW IT HELPS ME FEEL
AFTERNOON		
EVENING UNWIND		
EMERGENCY MOMENT		

Your night-time routine

A night-time routine helps create a gentle transition from the busyness of the day to restful sleep. Without a consistent routine, the mind and body may struggle to fully unwind, making it harder to relax and fall asleep. Establishing calming habits – such as reducing screen time, engaging in quiet activities and practising mindfulness – helps signal to the brain that it's time to slow down. A structured approach ensures that rest becomes intentional rather than an afterthought, supporting both physical relaxation and mental wellbeing. Over time, an evening routine can lead to better sleep, reduced stress and a greater balance.

A night-time routine is an opportunity to unwind and transition into rest. Creating a calming environment – such as dimming the lights and reducing screen time – helps signal to the body that it's time to relax. Gentle activities like sipping warm tea, practising deep breathing or light stretching can ease tension from the day. Engaging in a quiet practice, such as reading or

journaling, allows the mind to slow down. Taking a moment to reflect on a positive thought or gratitude can further promote a sense of peace. With consistency, a night-time routine becomes a way to support wellbeing and encourage restful sleep.

Tiny habits for your night-time routine

MAKE A LIST OF SIMPLE ACTIVITIES THAT HELP YOU FEEL RELAXED.

Take a moment to reflect on what your evening self-care can look like, so you never run out of inspiration.

SET AN EVENING ALARM TO REMIND YOURSELF IT'S TIME TO MINDFULLY SWITCH OFF FOR THE DAY.

This will remind you that it's time to start unwinding and help you to stick to a consistent routine.

DEDICATE 10 MINUTES TO DO ALL THE THINGS THAT WILL HELP YOU HAVE AN EASY MORNING.

Set out clean clothes for tomorrow and get your bag ready so you don't have to rush in the morning.

TAKE SOME TIME TO RECAP AND REFLECT ON WHAT HAS HAPPENED DURING YOUR DAY.

Check in with yourself and your emotions. What went well? What can you make better for tomorrow?

PREPARE YOUR BODY FOR A DEEPLY RESTFUL NIGHT.

Take a moment to relax your body by stretching, enjoying a warm shower or applying lotion with a calming scent.

CALM YOUR MIND FOR A PEACEFUL NIGHT OF REST.

Read a few pages of a book you love – something calming, not stimulating.

NURTURE YOUR SOUL WITH TRANQUILLITY BEFORE DRIFTING INTO SLEEP.

Repeat a calming affirmation, such as: 'I am at peace. I deserve rest. Tomorrow is a fresh start.'

Your night self-care plan

Having a night routine shouldn't feel like a list of tasks you must complete just to achieve a sense of accomplishment or a set of chores. Instead, think of it

SELF-CARE AREA	MIND
WHAT DO I CURRENTLY DO?	
CAN I IMPROVE THIS PRACTICE?	
THREE NEW NIGHT SELF-CARE IDEAS I WANT TO TRY:	

as a chance to include activities that bring you more relaxation and peace. A calm moment in your day to set the stage for deep rest, allowing your body, mind and soul to unwind.

Use this space to help you create a calming ritual that works for you:

BODY	SOUL

Self-care plan for tough days

A self-care plan for tough days is like a soft landing when everything feels heavy. It's not about fixing everything, it's about having a few comforting steps ready to guide you when your energy is low or your heart feels tired. The beauty of this kind of plan is in preparing it before the hard moments arrive, so when a tough day comes, you don't have to think – you just follow. Soft clothes, a quiet space, a warm drink or reaching out to someone you trust – these simple actions can hold you gently when the world feels too loud. It's a way of showing up for yourself with kindness, even when you're not at your strongest.

Tiny habits to get through a tough day

START WITH ONE GENTLE TASK, LIKE BRUSHING YOUR TEETH OR OPENING A WINDOW.

Doing just one small thing can help you feel a little more present and remind you that you've already begun.

GET DRESSED IN SOMETHING SOFT AND COMFORTING.

Even if you're staying home, a change of clothes can shift your mood and bring a sense of care.

MAKE A LIST WITH JUST ONE OR TWO TINY GOALS.

Choose things that feel doable – like making tea, replying to one message or stepping outside for five minutes.

MOVE YOUR BODY IN A WAY THAT FEELS KIND.

Stretch your arms, walk to the end of the street or put on a song and sway – small movements can help shift heavy feelings.

CHOOSE ONE SMALL ACTIVITY THAT BRINGS YOU A TINY SPARK OF JOY.

Watch something soothing, water your plants, colour, bake, cuddle a pet – let yourself do these things without guilt.

CELEBRATE THE LITTLE THINGS YOU DO.

Each time you complete something – no matter how small – say 'that was enough'. Because it truly is.

Your tough days' self-care plan

Even on the hard days, you are still worthy of care. This plan isn't about doing more, it's about having a soft place to land. When energy is low or everything feels like too much, this is your gentle guide – a few small habits that can hold you steady when the world feels shaky. Preparing it in advance means you don't have to decide in the moment; you can simply follow what you've already lovingly chosen for yourself. You can think of these little moments as threads that keep you connected – to comfort, to calm and to yourself.

WHEN I FEEL..	I CAN TRY...	WHY THIS HELPS ME
Overwhelmed and don't know where to start		
Disconnected or numb		
Stuck in my thoughts		
Lonely or in need of comfort		
Sad or low energy		

embracing imperfection

Embracing imperfection is one of the kindest things you can do for yourself. It means letting go of the idea that you need to have it all figured out, look a certain way or always get things right. Instead, you make space for your humanity – for the messiness, the pauses, the do-overs. You begin to see that the real beauty is in showing up anyway, learning gently and letting things be a little rough around the edges. Perfection isn't where growth lives – self-compassion is. And every time you choose progress over perfection, softness over shame and curiosity over criticism, you build a life rooted in truth and love. Apply this mindset to your self-care plans so that they stay flexible and forgiving – able to shift with your energy and needs, not hold you to rigid standards. Because care isn't about doing things perfectly; it's about showing up, gently, again and again.

Being gentle with yourself

Use these prompts to gently explore how you relate to imperfection in your self-care and daily life. There's no right or wrong way to answer – just let your thoughts flow with honesty and kindness. Write as much or as little as you need.

1. **WHAT WOULD MY SELF-CARE LOOK LIKE IF I LET GO OF NEEDING TO 'DO IT RIGHT' TODAY?**

....

....

....

2. WHERE HAVE I GROWN THIS YEAR, EVEN IF THE JOURNEY WASN'T PERFECT?

....

....

....

....

3. HOW CAN I BE KIND TO MYSELF WHEN I DON'T MEET MY OWN EXPECTATIONS?

....

....

....

....

THIS IS YOUR REMINDER THAT...

- Taking care of your mind is just as vital as taking care of your body.

- Self-care isn't selfish; it's essential for both your mental and physical health.

- Your worth as an individual is not tied to your productivity.

- Establishing your boundaries is a lifelong process.

- If your best is 50 per cent and you give 50 per cent, you have given 100 per cent for that day.

WHAT IS SOMETHING I'VE BEEN CARRYING LATELY – MENTALLY, EMOTIONALLY, OR PHYSICALLY – AND HOW MIGHT I BEGIN TO LET IT GO OR SHARE ITS WEIGHT?

WHAT HAS BEEN QUIETLY SHAPING ME RECENTLY, EVEN IF I HAVEN'T FULLY ACKNOWLEDGED IT YET?

A THOUGHT, A HABIT, A PERSON, OR A SHIFT IN PERSPECTIVE?

WHERE IN MY LIFE AM I LONGING FOR MORE CONNECTION, CLARITY, OR CALM – AND WHAT SMALL STEP COULD I TAKE TOWARD THAT TODAY?

RECALL A MOMENT TODAY OR RECENTLY WHEN YOU FELT FULLY PRESENT. WHAT WERE YOU DOING, WHAT DID YOU NOTICE WITH YOUR SENSES?

References

[1] Dalton-Smith, S. (2017). *Sacred rest: Recover your life, renew your energy, restore your sanity.* Hachette Book Group.

[2] Naczenski, L. M., De Vries, J. D., van Hooff, M. L. M., & Kompier, M. a. J. (2017). Systematic review of the association between physical activity and burnout. *Journal of Occupational Health, 59*(6), 477–494. doi.org/10.1539/joh.17-0050-ra

[3] Albulescu, P., Macsinga, I., Rusu, A., Sulea, C., Bodnaru, A., & Tulbure, B. T. (2022). 'Give me a break!' A systematic review and meta-analysis on the efficacy of micro-breaks for increasing well-being and performance. *PLoS ONE, 17*(8), e0272460. doi.org/10.1371/journal.pone.0272460

[4] Herbst, R., Sump, C., & Riddle, S. (2023). Staying in bounds: A framework for setting workplace boundaries to promote physician wellness. *Journal of Hospital Medicine, 18*(12), 1139–1143. doi.org/10.1002/jhm.13102

[5] Boettcher, J., Åström, V., Påhlsson, D., Schenström, O., Andersson, G., & Carlbring, P. (2013). Internet-Based Mindfulness Treatment for Anxiety Disorders: A randomized controlled trial. *Behavior Therapy*, 45(2), 241 253. doi.org/10.1016/j.beth.2013.11.003

[6] Creswell, J. D., Pacilio, L. E., Lindsay, E. K., & Brown, K. W. (2014). Brief mindfulness meditation training alters psychological and neuroendocrine responses to social evaluative stress. *Psychoneuroendocrinology*, *44*, 1–12. doi.org/10.1016/j.psyneuen.2014.02.007

[7] Black, D. S., O'Reilly, G. A., Olmstead, R., Breen, E. C., & Irwin, M. R. (2015). Mindfulness meditation and improvement in sleep quality and daytime impairment among older adults with sleep disturbances. *JAMA Internal Medicine*, *175*(4), 494. doi.org/10.1001/jamainternmed.2014.8081

[8] Egan, S. J., Rees, C. S., Delalande, J., Greene, D., Fitzallen, G., Brown, S., Webb, M., & Finlay-Jones, A. (2021). A review of self-compassion as an active ingredient in the prevention and treatment of anxiety and depression in young people.

Administration and Policy in Mental Health and Mental Health Services Research, 49(3), 385–403. doi.org/10.1007/s10488-021-01170-2

[9] Kirschner, H., Kuyken, W., Wright, K., Roberts, H., Brejcha, C., & Karl, A. (2019). Soothing your heart and feeling connected: A new experimental paradigm to study the benefits of self-compassion. *Clinical Psychological Science, 7*(3), 545–565. doi.org/10.1177/2167702618812438

[10] Neff, K. (2003). Self-compassion: an alternative conceptualization of a healthy attitude toward oneself. *Self and Identity, 2*(2), 85–101. doi.org/10.1080/15298860309032

[11] Homan, K. J., & Sirois, F. M. (2017). Self-compassion and physical health: Exploring the roles of perceived stress and health-promoting behaviors. *Health Psychology Open, 4*(2). doi.org/10.1177/2055102917729542

About the Author

Sofia Pellaschiar holds an MSc in Psychological Studies with Mental Health from the University of Aberdeen and an MSc in Foundations of Clinical Psychology from the University of Southampton. She is currently pursuing a PhD in Cognitive Neuroscience at Oxford Brookes University, focusing on mental health. Sofia is the founder of *My Self-Love Supply*, an Instagram platform with over 3 million followers, dedicated to promoting accessible self-care practices. Her first book, *The Morning Journal*, was a self-published success, and her previous, *A Hug in a Book*, offers a gentle approach to self-care habits and wellbeing.

POP PRESS

UK | USA | Canada | Ireland | Australia
India | New Zealand | South Africa

Pop Press is part of the Penguin Random House group of companies whose addresses can be found at
global.penguinrandomhouse.com

Penguin Random House UK
One Embassy Gardens, 8 Viaduct Gardens, London SW11 7BW

penguin.co.uk
global.penguinrandomhouse.com

First published by Pop Press in 2026

1

Copyright © Pop Press 2026
Illustrations © 2026

The moral right of the author has been asserted.

No part of this book may be used or reproduced in any manner for the purpose of training artificial intelligence technologies or systems. In accordance with Article 4(3) of the DSM Directive 2019/790, Penguin Random House expressly reserves this work from the text and data mining exception.

Text: Sofia Pellaschiar
Design: Georgie Hewitt
Illustrations: Kaitlyn Colormehappii
Editorial Director: Samantha Crisp
Editorial Assistant: Emille Bwale

Colour origination by Born Group
Printed and bound in China by C&C Offset Printing Co., Ltd.

The authorised representative in the EEA is Penguin Random House Ireland, Morrison Chambers,
32 Nassau Street, Dublin D02 YH68.

A CIP catalogue record for this book is available from the British Library

ISBN 9781529964813

MIX
Paper | Supporting
responsible forestry
FSC® C018179

Penguin Random House is committed to a sustainable future for our business, our readers and our planet. This book is made from Forest Stewardship Council® certified paper.